Sports

JOKES

By **Hugh Moore**

BIG BUDDY

JOKES

Big Buddy Books
An imprint of Abdo Publishing
abdopublishing.com

abdopublishing.com

Published by Abdo Publishing, a division of ABDO, PO Box 398166, Minneapolis, Minnesota 55439.
Copyright © 2017 by Abdo Consulting Group, Inc. International copyrights reserved in all countries.
No part of this book may be reproduced in any form without written permission from the publisher.
Big Buddy Books™ is a trademark and logo of Abdo Publishing.

Printed in the United States of America, North Mankato, Minnesota.
082016
012017

Illustrations: Sunny Grey/Spectrum Studio

Coordinating Series Editor: Tamara L. Britton
Contributing Editor: Katie Lajiness
Graphic Design: Taylor Higgins

Publisher's Cataloging-in-Publication Data

Names: Moore, Hugh, author.
Title: Sports jokes / by Hugh Moore.
Description: Minneapolis, MN : Abdo Publishing, 2017. | Series: Big buddy jokes
Identifiers: LCCN 2016944870 | ISBN 9781680785173 (lib. bdg.) | ISBN
    9781680798777 (ebook)
Subjects: LCSH: Sports--Juvenile humor. | Wit and humor--Juvenile humor.
Classification: DDC 818/.602--dc23
LC record available at http://lccn.loc.gov/2016944870

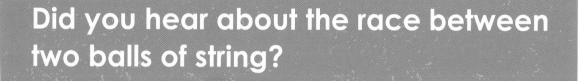

3

Bad-minton!

4

What did they call Dracula when he won the game?

The champ-ire!

What do dogs and baseball players have in common?

They both catch flies, chase strays, and run for home when they see the catcher!

Where do surfers sleep?

In water beds!

Why didn't the hockey player like to fish?

He kept getting called for hooking!

Why did the ballerina quit?

Because it was tutu hard!

Why did the tennis player's ears hurt?

Because of all the racquet!

Why did the witches call off their baseball game?

They couldn't find their bats!

7

Why are basketball players like babies?

Both dribble and can't walk!

How do hockey players pay for things at the store?

With checks!

What do you get when you cross a karate expert with a pig?

Pork chops!

How do hens encourage their football teams?

They egg them on!

What is the difference between a boxer and a person with a cold?

One knows his blows, and the other blows his nose!

What position does a ghost play in soccer?

Ghoulie!

Why did the golfer keep two pairs of pants in his golf bag?

In case he got a hole in one!

What did the basketball player ask the genie?

To grant him three swishes!

What does a pickle say when she wants to play cards?

Dill me in!

Why did the wrestlers play in the dark?

Their matches wouldn't light!

Where do football players dance?

At a foot-ball!

What is a baseball bat's favorite music?

Swing!

What kind of seafood does a wrestler like to eat?

Mussels!

What do you call a crab that plays baseball?

A pinch hitter!

Why didn't the dog want to play football?

It was a boxer!

Why couldn't the chicken get to first base?

It only hit fowl balls!

Why was Cinderella a bad basketball player?

Because her coach was a pumpkin!

What stories do basketball players tell?

Tall tales!

Why didn't the first baseman dance with Cinderella?

He missed the ball!

What did the bumblebee say when she made a shot?

Hive scored!

Why did the ballerina wear a tutu?

Because a one-one was too small and a three-three was too large.

What do you call it when a dinosaur slides into home plate?

A dino-score!

What dog would you want on your football team?

A golden receiver!

Where do old bowling balls end up?

In the gutter!

What did the gymnastic team do when their coach was late for the meet?

They flipped out!

Why did the campers bring a baseball player with them?

To pitch the tent!

What kind of tea do soccer players drink?

Penal-Tea.

Why was Cinderella thrown off the basketball team?

Because she ran away from the ball!

Why did the vegetarians stop swimming?

Because they didn't like meets.

What is a cheerleader's favorite drink?

Root beer.

What is a runner's favorite subject in school?

Jog-raphy!

Why were the bowling pins happy?

Because the bowling ball cleared them with room to spare!

What sport do hair stylists love the most?

Curling.

What is the hardest part about skydiving?

The ground!

What's a golfer's favorite letter?

Tee!

Why couldn't the bike stand up on its own?

It was two tired.

Why are stadium seats so cold?

Because fans sit in them!

Why was the baseball player arrested?

She kept stealing bases!

A tennis ball!

What did the volleyball player name her dog?

Spike!

Why shouldn't you tell jokes while ice-skating?

The ice might crack up!

How do you feel after playing a game with Dracula?

Drained!

What is the biggest diamond in the world?

A baseball diamond!

Which insect didn't make the football team?

The fumble bee!

What does a hockey player have in common with a magician?

Both do hat tricks!

What kind of cats bowl?

Alley cats!

Why are spiders good baseball players?

Because they catch flies!

WEBSITES

To learn more about Big Buddy Jokes, visit **booklinks.abdopublishing.com**. These links are routinely monitored and updated to provide the most current information available.